OUR TRIP WITH
CHILDHOOD CANCER
WITH Jesus
AT THE WHEEL

MICHAEL BLACK

WESTBOW
PRESS®
A DIVISION OF THOMAS NELSON
& ZONDERVAN

WestBow Press books may be ordered through booksellers or by contacting:

WestBow Press
A Division of Thomas Nelson & Zondervan
1663 Liberty Drive
Bloomington, IN 47403
www.westbowpress.com
1 (866) 928-1240

ISBN: 978-1-9736-1839-3 (sc)
ISBN: 978-1-9736-1838-6 (e)

Print information available on the last page.

WestBow Press rev. date: 01/31/2018

Dedication

To my wife, Karel for keeping journals
throughout the journey
&
This book is dedicated to my family and
friends that helped us remain strong,
&
to the Doctors and Nurses of Cardinal Glennon
Children's Hospital in St. Louis, Missouri
for their knowledge and compassion,
&
To the children, parents and families that are on
their own journey with this terrible disease,
&
Most of all to my daughter Kayla,
for being Daddy's little girl!!!!

Foreword

By Clayton Black

As Kayla's older brother, I always felt that it was my responsibility to look after her. I felt that responsibility on her first day of Kindergarten when we got on the school bus together. We played "school time" that whole summer before so I could make sure she was prepared for her big day. She always grew pretty weary of my subpar teaching skills and would often quit on me. Fortunately, as you are about to find out, that was about the only thing Kayla Faye Black ever quit.

As we grew up, we challenged each other. I could not let her outdo me and set fairly high academic expectations. Kayla had the same teachers just a few years behind me and I think they'll all agree that she not only met those expectations, she exceeded them. In addition to being a straight-A student, she was her class president, a hard worker and an exemplary role model for her classmates.

Having seen what college life was like through four

years at Southern Illinois University- Carbondale, I felt a responsibility to look after her when she was planning for college herself. True to her faith, she chose Greenville College to wrap up her Elementary education degree. Choosing a Christian college definitely alleviated my concerns.

I assumed I was handing over many of my responsibilities when I stood next to her wonderful fiancé and now-husband as a member of her wedding party on June 24, 2017. As I've grown up and faced some of my own challenges, I now realize that we share those responsibilities and now look out for each other.

Although, I have heard this story read in our church and at our annual Relay for Life, reading the pages that follow were not particularly comfortable. I try not to let my brain wander into some of those what ifs. What if my family had not packed up my sister and taken her to St. Louis? What if they were not led to the steady hands of Dr. Silan or the reassuring and determined voice of Dr. Chu? What if my family had not had our faith in God and had a support network of family, friends and ministers to help them through those difficult times? Fortunately, we'll never know the answer to those questions.

The story that follows is a true story about a family's battle with childhood cancer. Although it's my family's story, I think this same story is playing out everywhere in this world with thousands of loving parents, grandparents, and siblings on the same journey, going to hospitals and sitting in waiting rooms- not knowing what the next x-ray or blood test is going to reveal.

I think my father felt compelled to tell this story to give those families hope that there is a happy ending. When you're stuck in the day to day grind of the journey, it can be hard to keep your faith in God and think that one day, you'll see your child get on the school bus and eventually graduate and go off to college and then walk down the aisle and get married, someday starting a family of their own.

I hope that Dad's story will serve as a glimmer of hope for those families to know that they are not alone. Relying on your support network, listening to your intuition and most importantly keeping your faith in God helped my family get through an incredibly difficult time and hopefully it will help those families as well.

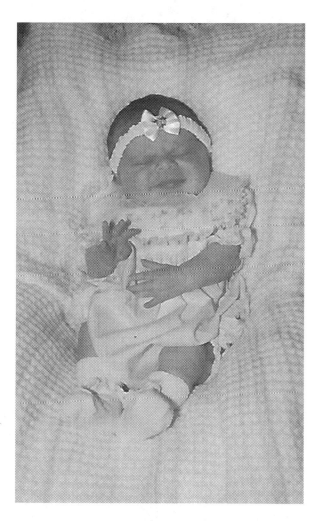

Kayla at three weeks of age

My wife Karel started having contractions on the evening of January 8. We decided it was time to head to the hospital. God was blessing us with a baby daughter. Kayla Faye Black was born on January 9, 1995 in Robinson, IL at a small county hospital. The birth came with no complications. Our whole family including our other child, Clayton, then six years' old was there to welcome her into the world. It was a day that completed our family. Everyone joked that she had her dad's eyes and her mom's smile. She was a beautiful little baby girl.

The first six weeks of our lives were like that of any other parents of a new born baby. Kayla was 6 pounds and 15 ounces when she was born. Although that was a lower birth weight than our son, it was not a reason for concern. What began to be cause for concern, however, was that she was struggling to gain weight. On a night in mid-February, after being gone all evening, we arrived home. I warmed a bottle for our baby girl. While I was feeding her, I noticed she felt very warm. After she drank the bottle, I placed her on my shoulder and started patting her back. As I brought her down from my shoulder, I noticed a spot of blood on the cloth diaper I was using as a burp cloth. I looked in her mouth to see where the blood was coming from and noticed a small hole in her upper left gum. I figured it was some kind of abscess, so I told my wife I would take her over to the hospital to be checked while she stayed at home with our son since it was starting to get late. By the time I got her all bundled up and drove a short distance to the hospital, the left side of her face was starting to swell up even further.

The emergency room doctor came in and started his examination. What started as an examination slowly turned into an interrogation. He started asking me questions that were leading to allegations of child abuse. I replied to him that I had done nothing wrong to her. He continued his line of questioning, asking whether the baby had been dropped. He asked if there were siblings in the house that could have inadvertently injured her. The questioning moved on to my wife and why she was not there. I explained to him that she was home with our son. He demanded that she needed to be at the hospital, so we could get to the bottom of this.

While all the accusations were made, I calmly denied each one. It would have been very easy to become angry with the accusations, but I knew that Kayla needed me, and I knew in my heart that she was the primary concern. Whatever happened to me, I had no control over. I said a prayer to God to help me remain strong, to keep the strength and my faith. God said in Psalm 22:19, "But you, LORD, do not be far from me. You are my strength; come quickly to help me."

While sitting in the exam room, I overheard the doctor directing the on-duty nurse to call the Robinson Police Department. I became very upset and made a phone call home. I asked my wife to get to the hospital as soon as possible. Worrying that there was a possibility of being arrested, I wanted her at the hospital to be with our daughter. He stated to the nurse it was a case of child abuse. Having worked part-time at the local ambulance service, I knew several of the hospital staff. Fortunately, the nurse told the doctor she knew me from working together and she could not see me doing anything to Kayla. She reasoned with him to wait for blood work and x-rays to be done before calling in the law.

A lab technician came in and performed a blood draw on Kayla and shortly after an x-ray technician took her for a facial x-ray. The results from the x-ray were negative for fractures, however the blood test results indicated an extremely high white cell count showing an infection. It was decided to admit her and start antibiotic I.V. therapy. They also did a blood culture and it was later determined that she had a streptococcus infection.

Her doctor came in the next morning and decided to conduct an MRI. The test revealed a large area of infection throughout the entire left side of her face. Her skin had swollen even further from the day before and was looking white and fluffy like a pillow. My wife and I both felt that something did not seem right. We were told the swelling was more than likely a result of the fluids they were giving her. Good friends of ours that worked with the county ambulance, visited with us the next day. They warned us that the small local hospital was not equipped to care for infants and to not stay in Robinson too long if she didn't start to show improvement. They said that we should not hesitate to ask for her to be transferred to a children's hospital.

Kayla began showing small signs of improvement, so she was sent home after three days and provided with home care. We had a nurse stopping by three times a day and administering her I.V. antibiotics. After five days, Kayla had tired of this routine and took matters into her own hands, deciding to pull out her I.V. line. I made a call to the doctor's office and explained to him what was going on. He ordered more blood tests to see if her infection was clearing up. The blood test revealed her white cell count was 27,000, around twice the normal level for an infant. I expressed my concern to her doctor and he assured me that it was coming down. After talking it over with my wife, we took our friends' recommendations from a few days earlier and requested a second opinion. The doctor offered to refer us to Riley's Children's Hospital in Indianapolis, Indiana. One step ahead of him, I had already been researching it with my insurance company and found they were not covered through our insurance.

We told him we wanted to take Kayla to Cardinal Glennon Children's Hospital in St. Louis. A power from above was guiding my wife and me to take her somewhere else and telling us that the small county hospital was just not equipped to give Kayla the help she needed. We had family that utilized Cardinal Glennon in recent years and they were very happy with the care their children had received. So, we are hoping the direction that God was pointing us in, would get us the help we needed. The doctor left the room and made the call. When he came back in the room, he told us they would see her and to take her through the Emergency Room. We picked up our son from school, went home and loaded up the car.

Somebody was telling us to pack a suitcase. We were scared for Kayla. We had no idea what would be found. We were prepared to place her in God's hands to find out what was wrong. We had a feeling deep inside us that it was not good, but we were putting our trust in God to get the answers we were looking for. Jeremiah 17:14 says, "Heal me, O Lord, and I will be healed; save me and I will be saved, for you are the one I praise."

So, on February 27th we headed out on the three-hour drive to St. Louis, stopping on the way and dropping off Clayton at my parent's house in St. Elmo, IL. We arrived at Cardinal Glennon Children's Hospital at around 5:00 pm. After a short period of time, a nurse came out and took us back to an exam room. She started her initial assessment, taking Kayla's blood pressure in both arms and both legs. At this point, we looked at each other and realized that this was the first time throughout this entire ordeal that Kayla had her blood pressure taken and she was getting it taken in both arms and legs. A doctor came in and introduced himself as an associate professor of renal functions at St. Louis University. He conducted his thorough examination and looked at the numbers the nurse had documented.

He told us that Kayla had either a renal issue, cardiac issue or both. He explained that her blood pressure was 180 systolic and that normal in infants was 100 or under. Medications were immediately started on Kayla to bring her blood pressure down. Only after the medications were administered were we told that 180 systolic was a level so dangerous that a stroke could have occurred. The doctor then ordered a spinal puncture to test her spinal fluid and check her white cell count. It came back extremely elevated, indicating the possibility of bacterial meningitis. Over the course of a couple hours, it was becoming clear that God led us to the right place to figure out what was wrong with our baby girl.

Kayla was admitted to the hospital's Transitional Care Unit (TCU) at 2:00 am. Hospital policy only allowed one parent to stay the night with her. I was fortunate to have my brother living only 20 minutes away, so I was able to stay with him. When I arrived back at the hospital, it seemed like reality had set in. Our adventure had begun.

They had her on a cardiac monitor, I.V., and Pulse Oximeter. They had her already set up for both a renal and heart ultrasound. We knew that something serious was going on during the renal ultrasound. There were several doctors coming in and observing the test.

After getting back to her room a new doctor came in. His name was Dr. Chu. Dr. Chu was the Professor of Oncology at St. Louis University School of Medicine. He shared with us the devastating news that the renal ultrasound had revealed a tumor on her left adrenal gland. He said that he did not feel that the tumor that had been located was malignant, but that surgery would be required to remove the tumor. Dr. Chu shared this information with such compassion and tenderness for Kayla and us and eased the blow of receiving such awful news. He added that her heart was enlarged, and her diaphragm had thickened as a result of the infection which meant the infection would have to be controlled before surgery could occur.

Our dear friend and minister Dean West came over and prayed with us. He told us that God was in control and would guide the doctors in caring for Kayla. I had to go back home to take care of my work schedule at the correctional facility that I worked at. My supervisor and friend, Gary Wyant, went out of his way to get me the needed time off from work to be able to be with my family. I also spoke with my parents on the way home. My father was able to take time off to move into our house an hour and a half from his to keep my son in school and provide as close to a normal life for him as possible. Little did I know that this adventure was only in the beginning stages.

When I arrived back at the hospital the next day, they had started further testing. Kayla's blood test results revealed that her cortisol level was three times normal. The doctor explained to us the reason for this was that the body knew there was a problem and it was over-producing to combat what was going on with the tumor and the infection. The high level contributed to her heart enlarging and her diaphragm thickening. This was also the reason for the cushioning of her skin which we had already noticed.

Prior to doing the surgery, they wanted a better look

at her tumor. The decided to do an M.R.I. Medication was administered to relax her for the test. Due to her high cortisol level, the medication had an opposite effect on her. Kayla became very combative. It just breaks one's heart to see your baby going through all of this. She had more blood tests that showed her infection had finally cleared up, so surgery was set for March 3.

The day had come for surgery. Kayla had been moved to a different room with a little boy named Eric, who was just a little older than she was. He had numerous health concerns. His mother was very open to talking, far more than we were. All we could do was worry about the surgery the doctors were preparing to perform. At one point, Eric's mother had to step out for a bit. While she was gone, Eric stopped breathing. A team came into the room and got him resuscitated. Watching this happen just hours before Kayla's surgery was heartbreaking. Just thinking that the little girl we had grown to love and had in our lives for less than two months was about to go through a procedure most people live all their lives without having to go through was too much for either of us to process.

The operating room staff came to pick her up for surgery at 12:15 pm. They were kind enough to allow us to carry her to the operating room entrance. One of the hardest things we ever did was to hand off our sweet baby girl to them and watch the double doors close behind them as they walked down the hall with her. I dropped to my knees in tears asking God to be with her and the surgeons and everyone that would be involved in removing the tumor from our baby girl. Today, I think about Deuteronomy 31:6. It says, "Be strong and courageous. Do not be afraid or terrified because of them, for the LORD your God goes with you; he will never leave you nor forsake you." God never left my side or my family's side that day.

Karel went to the waiting room and got my dad to come help me up. I did not want to get up. I was so worried and could not walk away. Dad helped me up and hugged me and walked with me to the waiting room. I found a lot of family there who had come to be by our side on the day that we needed them the most. My dad and mom had brought Clayton so we all could be together as a family. Also there, was my dad's brother Eugene, who was a Methodist minister and Pastor Greg Courtright who was the minister of our previous church before we moved to Robinson. Many of our family friends and my coworkers from work were there also. My Uncle Eugene gave one of the sweetest prayers that could ever be said. He was like the voice of a savior speaking to us. After his prayer, he gave me a hug and looked me in the eye and told me that God has a special purpose for Kayla. We all hugged together and cried together. God's power was at work in the room. It gave us a sense of comfort having loved ones close to us.

Dr. Chu came out of the operating room several times

throughout the surgery to keep us updated on what was happening. Undoubtedly, the hardest news he shared with us was that the small tumor that showed up on the CAT scan was part of a much larger tumor. Dr. Silan, who was the chief surgeon came out to talk to us. He was a very nice man that spoke with compassion in his voice. He told us that she would be going to the Intensive Care Unit (ICU). I asked him about the tumor. He said that it was egg shaped, gray in color, and was fully encapsulated. He also said that it was not attached to any other organs. He explained the surgery, saying they removed the tumor and her left adrenal gland. He said the tumor was attached to the adrenal vein. I asked him, "Is it cancerous," knowing it was the question whose answer we feared the most. If it were cancerous, it would have had the potential to spread to other parts of her body. Dr. Silan said because of the color and encapsulation, he did not feel it was malignant, but it would have to be checked by a Doctor of Pathology to make that assessment. He said that could take five days.

After they got Kayla to the ICU, we got to go in and see her. It was difficult to see her hooked up to all the monitors with wires and cords strung about and numbers flashing across the screens that she was surrounded by. She was heavily medicated and slept almost all evening. We stayed with her as long as they would allow us to. With her being in the ICU, there was no way that Karel and I could consider leaving the hospital that night. We decided to sleep in the waiting room. The next morning, we were able to go see her again. She was awake when we got in her room. Her blood pressure was still running high and her breathing tube and her feeding tube were still hooked up to her from the night before.

Since Cardinal Glennon is a Catholic Hospital, they had sleeping quarters that were previously used by nuns when the hospital was founded in 1956. They maintain these rooms and make them available to parents from out of town who want to stay close to their child for the night. Hospital staff assisted us in getting in one of these rooms. We were so grateful that we did not have to leave the hospital grounds. Something about falling asleep in the same building as Kayla gave us at least some level of comfort. The next morning, we woke up early and headed back to the ICU to find that they had removed Kayla's breathing and feeding tubes. Karel was so happy because she finally got to hold and feed her again. It was a good day! God was taking care of her. Many of the friends and family that had made the one to three-hour drive on surgery day came back again and spent time with us. The following day they transferred Kayla from the ICU to a regular room and it felt like things were finally starting to look up.

Kayla seemed like she was doing very well recuperating from the surgery. They discontinued her I.V. and started administering her medication through a port. Although she continued to show these signs of improvement, the hardest part for Karel and I was waiting on the results of the pathology, to determine whether the tumor was cancerous. Finally, five days after the surgery, Dr. Chu came into Kayla's room. He asked us to step across the hall to the conference room. He was always so positive, but I could tell from the tone of his voice that he had some bad news to share with us. He told us that the pathologist had determined that her tumor was cancerous, carcinoma in type. We both broke down.

Dr. Chu said that there was no treatment that could be done. He explained that chemotherapy, the treatment method that would be used to treat most patients, attacks the fastest growing cells in the body, which are typically cancer cells. But, because she is an infant, all her cells are fast growing, and she could not withstand it. He did say that he felt optimistic that given her age and her size, the cancer had not spread significantly. He said, "There are a lot of unknowns and unknowns are sometimes good".

We returned to her room in tears. Reality was setting in that we may lose our little girl. I called my parents and told them that we needed someone to help hold us together. After hanging up with my dad the phone rang, and it was our dear friend Nancy. I struggled for words to tell her our bad news. I could not talk and had to hang the phone up. Just a few minutes later, our friend and minister at the church we had been attending, Dean West called. Dean told me he had gotten a call from Nancy and she had told him that we needed him. He prayed with us over the phone. He told us that God loves us and he is in control. He said to keep our faith strong and continue to pray and God will listen. He said that members of his church would be praying all night for Kayla and that prayer chains all over the country had been activated on Kayla's behalf.

The next day, Dr. Chu came back in the room and told us he was up all-night reading articles on pediatric adrenal carcinoma cancer. He found a treatment program that was successful in Dallas, Texas on a two-year-old child. He said he wanted to watch her first before starting any treatment and although there are a lot of differences between a two-year-old and a two-month-old going through this treatment, he felt it was worth exploring. It was apparent that the prayers were helping. It felt as though God was hearing them and working through Dr. Chu to make sure he left no stone uncovered in finding a treatment plan for Kayla.

The following day we were still feeling upset but, trying to remain positive that they had removed all the cancer during the surgery. Kayla's blood pressure was finally starting to show some improvement and she was finally able to wear some of her own clothes, after being unhooked from everything. Soon after she was finally unhooked from most of the monitors, she started to show signs of getting a cold, so sure enough they started hooking her back up to the monitors. Poor Kayla had been through so much in the last couple weeks and just could not catch a break.

One of the doctors assigned to Kayla's case was Dr. Aceto. He was the Professor of Endocrinology at St. Louis University and was called in given the removal of one of Kayla's adrenal glands as part of the surgery. He came into the room and examined Kayla. After his examination, he asked us if they could do some video of her to use for educational purposes. We immediately said that we would not consent to it. After Dr. Aceto left the room, my wife and I sat down and had a talk about the videotaping. We talked about our privacy concerns, but we also talked about how Kayla's case could be used to save other children's lives. We asked our nurse to have Dr. Aceto come back to the room. We told him we would consent and agreed to provide them with some video we had already done at home. The hospital provided us with a copy of the final video. While

I still have it, I have only been able to watch it one time. I cannot watch the video without tears coming to my eyes. I remember later that night and every other night driving to my brother's house, having conversations with God. I was asking him for strength and guidance. Now I look back at Psalm 46-1, "God is our refuge and strength, an ever-present help in trouble". I also remember the words my uncle said in the waiting room during her surgery, "God has a special purpose for Kayla in life". I have now started to realize what he meant. I think God called on us to allow that video to be done.

The next day, Clayton came over with my parents. We took him out to see the sights of St. Louis, while my parents stayed with Kayla. I think he had enjoyed his last week and a half with grandpa, but at six-years old, it could not have been easy on him dealing with the confusion of why suddenly mom and dad had taken off to St. Louis with Kayla. We did our best to put on happy faces to remind him that we still loved him too. While we were out, the doctors had found that Kayla did not have a cold, but rather Respiratory Syncytial Virus, or RSV for short. They took out her central line but started a new I.V. to give her antibiotics and put her on oxygen. Just a few hours away from her bedside and it seemed like the world had come crashing down again.

We endured the RSV with her for the next five days. She was on so many different medications, throwing up everything that she took in. The decision was made by the doctors to take her off the steroid and watch her for a couple days. They told us that she would be watched for acute renal insufficiency syndrome.

To prepare for her to be at home, Karel and I were instructed on how to administer a steroid shot to Kayla. They said the reason for this was that by removing one of her two adrenal glands, the remaining adrenal gland was not producing at a sustainable level, so she had to be given hydrocortisone to maintain the same level that she was previously. She was still throwing up a lot of phlegm, but the doctors associated this with her continued recuperation from RSV. Once the severe symptoms from the RSV had passed, she was finally looking happy and was constantly smiling.

We were told that she would finally be going home on Monday, March 20. But Monday came, and she started having some more blood pressure problems. It jumped up to 140. So, the trip home was postponed. The next day she was not eating right and just wanted to sleep. Her doctors wanted to do more blood tests to check her cortisol level. After the blood tests, it was determined she needed placed on a hydrocortisone I.V. She still was not properly producing a sustainable level with her existing adrenal gland. The results were amazing. Within a matter of minutes of starting the I.V., she started acting happy again.

She continued to do well the next few days. Her only problem seemed the inability to keep all her oral medication down. There was so much of it though, that I am not sure how anyone could have kept it down. She was started on a Zantac I.V. to help her stomach. The doctors were thinking that the medications had irritated her stomach. It really helped a lot. Once again, we were able to leave the hospital for a while again to take our son shopping. It was important for us to make sure he felt the love of his Daddy and Mommy too. While we were out, we also managed to find an Easter bonnet for Kayla.

The new plan was for her to go home on Monday, March 27. We really hated to get our hopes up too much, we had been told that before only to suffer setbacks. I got Clayton picked up because it was important to him to get to help bring his sister home. We got to the hospital at 11:00 am. Finally, at 3:00 pm, they came in and told us she was for sure going home. Appointments were made to come back the following week for a visit to the Oncology/Hematology Clinic.

We packed our bags and headed out for home. Karel had not been home since we arrived in St. Louis to start this month-long journey exactly one month before and by this point, Kayla had spent nearly half of her brief life in a hospital bed. Home was such a sweet word to hear. In our minds we couldn't help but think to ourselves, what if the tumor returned? We couldn't let the "what ifs" run our lives. We were going to live every day to the fullest and cherish every day we had together. The Bible tells us in Matthew 6:34, "Therefore do not worry about tomorrow, for tomorrow will worry about itself. Each day has enough trouble of its own."

On our way home, we decided to stop and see Karel's Grandmother Faye. She had not been able to visit Kayla at the hospital due to her own fight with breast cancer. Kayla was named after her grandmother Faye. When Kayla was born we named her after her Grandmother Faye as sort of a tribute while she was battling cancer. Little did we realize how much irony there would be to this decision just a few months later. Karel's grandmother was surprised and delighted to see Kayla. It was such a great experience to get to see the smile on Grandma's face even though she was not feeling well herself. It was like it breathed new life into her.

Pulling down our street was such a surreal experience. Friends had lined the street to our driveway with balloons and welcome home signs to celebrate our return. We were so happy to be home. It never before seemed like such a wonderful place to be. When we arrived home around 6:30, we were met by our neighbor bringing us dinner. My mom came over to help get us settled back in and to help Karel the next day since I was scheduled to go back to work.

Never knew going to work would feel so good. Karel said the phone rang off the wall with friends calling, welcoming us back home. Karel's parents also came over and stayed till Clayton got home from school.

Kayla settled in and seemed to be doing extremely well. Her blood pressure was staying in normal range. We were taking it several times per day. The next day, Karel got to get out of the house and do normal things like grocery shopping and her haircut for the first time in a long time. Kayla was going to require constant care for a while so another one of Karel's decisions was to stop by her job and drop off her resignation letter. There would be plenty of opportunities for Karel to find new employment, but we both agreed we didn't want her spending time at a daycare or a baby sitter or anywhere except under her mom's care.

Cardinal Glennon Hospital found a pediatrician in Vincennes, Indiana, about 30 minutes from where we lived. The pediatrician had worked at Cardinal Glennon during his residency. They had sent us home with copies of all her hospital records to give to him on her first visit. I was thumbing through them and came across her discharge summary from the hospital. I read the statement, "The tumor has a poor history and is likely to return with a poor prognosis to the patient". Although we had known that all along, this was devastating to read. I knew I could not share this with my wife. It would have destroyed her.

It came the day for her first appointment with her new

primary care doctor. We were very happy to have a new pediatrician that would work with her doctors in St. Louis. They arranged it so that every time she saw one of them they would forward all of her information back and forth. After being home for five days, we decided it was time for the welcome home signs and balloons to come down. They had done their job. We felt the love that went into making the signs and hanging them.

The next day was going to be a birthday celebration for my Grandma Nell's 95th birthday in Patoka, Illinois. My side of the family is very large and each year, we would attend the small Methodist church that my grandmother attends and then throw a party for her afterwards. During the service, my grandmother's minister came to us and asked us to come up front. He told the church that the little girl that they had been praying so hard for was in church with them that morning. He asked to hold Kayla and walked around the church with her while the congregation sang "Jesus Loves Me". Tears flowed throughout the church. I saw people crying that I had never met before. I felt like I knew them and am sure they felt they knew us. It was quite evident that they had truly been praying for Kayla's health. We felt so blessed by God that morning, knowing that all of those people had been praying so hard for Kayla.

It was the first time my grandmother had gotten to see Kayla. My grandmother was a very spiritual person who held Jesus close to her heart and did not care much for material goods. I could tell that nobody had prayed any harder than her. God had rewarded her prayers that day by getting to meet and hold her great-granddaughter. After church, we had a dinner in my grandmother's honor. With everything we had been going through, it was so comforting to get to see the entire family. Kayla got to meet the entire family for the first time. We knew we still had a long road ahead and it was enlightening to take a break with loved ones if only for one afternoon.

Kayla meeting her Great Grandma Nell for the first time

Monday morning came around and it was back to reality. We got Clayton off to school and it was off on our 3-hour drive back to Cardinal Glennon Hospital for Kayla's first out-patient visit. She was to be seen by three different doctors. The visit was pretty routine. They checked her weight and incision. They did change her medication because her blood pressure is starting to stabilize. We are to keep a close eye on it and not give her medication unless it is necessary. They did not do any other tests, but made our next appointment for two weeks.

The next Monday, it was off to her pediatrician. He was very pleased. Kayla was finally starting to gain weight as she should. She was right at three months old and finally was weighing just over 9 pounds. He also told us now that since she was doing so well to go ahead with her baby shots, so, two days later we took her to the health department. Life all week seemed like as business as usual. She was hungry all the time. I guess she was just making up for all the lost time that she either couldn't eat or did not feel like eating.

Seemed like every Monday, we had another appointment, so off we were again to St. Louis. This appointment took a lot longer. It was a lot harder to go through. They had blood tests and chest x-rays scheduled. Dr. Chu explained the blood tests to us. He said that they use certain marker to determine tumor activity in the body. He said the marker they were using was set by a number prior to her surgery. We were told that they were hoping for a decline in that number. Any increase would show new tumor activity in the body. All the testing was scary for us. We prayed that her numbers would be good and that the x-ray would not reveal anything new. I remember Dr. Chu telling us that the unknowns were good, but they are unnerving as well. Every one of her tests came back good. To lighten the mood, Dr. Chu made a balloon animal for Clayton. Dr. Chu found his calling in life working with children.

Our next appointment was scheduled for two weeks later. The next two weeks were normal around the house, with Clayton settled back into his life and Kayla constantly continuing to improve every day. We felt that she was looking so much better that it was time to get some pictures. On the way, I got to meet a very nice IL State Trooper that rewarded me with my first ever speeding ticket. He thought I was special and gave me a $95 fine. All jokes aside, he also gave me a nice talking to. He told me I had very precious cargo in the back seat and I should be very careful with it. I smiled and agreed with him.

Only episode we experienced was Kayla running a fever one night. Clayton had been sick and evidently shared it with his sister. We even managed to get out of the house some, spending time visiting with friends.

Two weeks sure do fly by. It is already for our next trip to St. Louis. This trip we were scheduled to see the Endocrine doctor along with Dr. Chu. The visit went very well. More good news, Kayla got her hydrocortisone reduced and she got off the Zantac for her stomach. The hardest thing we endure back in St. Louis is not in the exam room, but in the waiting room. We are becoming so familiar with other parents. Some of the stories are not going as well as others. When you see a two-year-old child that has lost of their hair due to chemotherapy or you see a child that has target marks on their little heads where they are receiving radiation treatments, it just makes your heart sink. No child should have to endure what these children go through. She got her next appointment scheduled in two weeks again.

It really seems like time flies between appointments, but at the same time, we find comfort knowing, she is doing so good. In just a few days the phone rang, and it was Dr. Chu. He had great news for us. Kayla's blood test results were good, and he is going to start having Kayla's pediatrician do them soon. Our next appointment in St. Louis was a long one. They had her scheduled for a CT. The plan was to take a good look at the area where her tumor had been. They also took care of doing blood test. By the end of all of it that day, she was totally exhausted and so were we. We still had the long trip to make home. We called Dr. Chu the next day and got the news we wanted. Everything looked great with no sign of any new tumor growth. We also got the news that we are now going a month between visits. The next couple appointments went very well also. Everything pointed that Kayla was doing very well, better than many even expected. She is smiling and even laughing. She is feeling like a baby should. Kayla is continuing to gain weight.

During the August trip to Cardinal Glennon, we decided to take a trip up to the floor where Kayla spent the better part of a month of her life. We got to see so many of the nurses that provided care for her. Seeing them felt like a family reunion. We had gotten so close with several of them. There were many times they cried with us. Many of them also prayed with us.

On August 24th, Kayla got the diarrhea followed by vomiting. We called the pediatrician and he admitted her to the hospital. IV therapy was started to keep her from dehydrating. The also did some x-rays. To our relief and comfort, it was determined she just had a stomach virus along with a urinary tract infection. Her doctor decided to keep her in the hospital for a few days and send her home with medication. A follow-up with the doctor in a few days showed she was doing fine. Finally, Kayla was starting to stand up in her walker. She started throwing things and laughing. She is starting to scoot backwards on her tummy too. It is so cute and delightful to watch her knowing how far she has come since her diagnosis.

We had a scheduled appointment with her pediatrician on September 20th. We were shocked to find that she has gained a full pound since he last saw her. He is doing her blood test now to save having to go to St. Louis for them. The plan is for him to notify Dr. Chu of her levels to check tumor activity. Dr. Chu called us the next day and told us that everything was good. It called for a celebration, so we all went out for dinner.

On September 30th, we received a call that Karel's grandmother was in the hospital and all indications were that she was in her final hours of life. She was losing her battle with cancer. She had fought the battle so hard and had not given up. She was such a fighter. Karel headed out to see her at the hospital. Karel's father called us on Monday evening, October 2nd. Her grandmother had passed away at 5:40 pm.

While it is so sad, we know in our hearts that she is now pain free. You could tell that she was in extreme pain the last several months of her life, but she never complained to the people around her. It just saddens us that Kayla will not remember the grandmother she was named after. Clayton was so upset. He was so close to each of his grandmothers. We did send him to school the next day, but advised his teacher of our loss. She told us he settled in fine. Karel called home and arrangements had been made for her grandmother.

We headed over on Thursday for the visitation. We were surrounded by family. This was Clayton's first experience losing a grandparent that he could remember. With him only being six, it is hard to make him understand life and death. We had to be careful in explaining it. We really did not want him to know about her battle with cancer. We had to separate Karel's grandmother and Kayla. We had explained to him that his sister had cancer. We couldn't let him think that everyone that gets cancer dies. He was very upset when he saw her in the casket. The next day we went to a family dinner and to the funeral to say our final goodbyes.

It was not only rough on Clayton, but it was hard for Karel as well. She grew up only a couple miles away from her. She spent a lot of time on their farm growing up. Yet, Karel is taking comfort knowing she is no longer suffering from that terrible disease that took her life.

The next day was yet another trip to St. Louis to see Kayla's doctors. This was scheduled to be a long appointment. They had her set up for a CT. She had to go through an IV and contrast to get a good image of her kidneys. The test did not take too long but it took two hours to get her awake from the sedative they had given her. We got bittersweet news from the test. Though the test did not reveal any tumor activity, it did reveal that her left kidney was substantially smaller. They explained that this was largely due to the removal of the adrenal gland on that side and the gland normally sets on top of the kidney. They were not highly concerned, but they did say it was not properly functioning. They said her other kidney would do the work. The doctor is concerned about her left eye. The eye appears to be larger and is very watery. They want to watch it and be proactive if necessary.

As time passed, Kayla continued to show progress, getting active and starting to verbalize things. She really seems attached to saying Da-Da. The holidays were coming near and naturally the whole family was getting excited. After the year we had been through, we were just happy to know that we were going to be able to celebrate a holiday season with Kayla. It was so much fun, getting the kids ready for Halloween. This was Kayla's first Halloween and we dressed her up like a little pumpkin.

We had not seen some of the family for quite some time. My family always gets together to celebrate Thanksgiving. We had not seen a lot of them since my grandmother's birthday in April when Kayla had just gotten out of the hospital. Everyone was so shocked to see how well she was doing and how much she had changed. She was starting to say a lot more things like mom-mom, mama and papa.

We felt like things were going really well till the following week, Kayla had another round of vomiting and was admitted again to the hospital. They made three attempts to start an I.V. with no luck and eventually started her on Pedialyte. Kayla couldn't keep anything down. Our doctor was not initially available that was familiar with Kayla. The doctor that saw her did not realize she only had one adrenal gland. I had to explain to the doctor that she was at risk for acute renal insufficiency syndrome which we had heard from our doctors throughout the previous spring and summer. They then gave her a blood test to check her level and found that she had Ribozyme Gastro Virus. Most people and even infants do not have issues with the virus, but Kayla's immune system had been compromised from the cancer and removal of her adrenal gland that it was causing her problems.

By the next day, Kayla had improved, and the doctor said she could go home. Given our weekend at the hospital, our trip to Cardinal Glennon Hospital needed to be rescheduled. We did not want to take any chances exposing the other children there to Kayla's virus as their immune systems were likely in a similar position as Kayla's. We rescheduled her appointment for the following week.

The next Monday, we made the long trip across the state toward St. Louis. It was a long appointment. She had a chest x-ray and blood work along with a thorough examination. All tests came back good. We were so happy that she did not have to go back until March for another CT. It was only a week before Christmas. Christmas preparations started around our house. The tree was up, cookies and candy made, and presents all wrapped. This was going to be a Christmas like no other. There was so much to look back at and to be thankful to God for over the past year.

We spent Christmas Eve with my parents, my brother and my Grandma Meyer. That evening, we went to Karel's parents' house for dinner and gift exchange. It was so important to be with those that stood by our side and shared their love with us, providing their comfort to us during our difficult year. We did not spend the night on this trip. We wanted to wake up together as a family on Christmas morning in our house with the presents under the tree and a fire in the fireplace.

On Christmas morning, Clayton had already wandered into the living room and found that Santa had already visited the house by 3:00 am and wanted to get up and see what he had brought. We convinced him to wait until at least 6:00 am. Both Clayton and Kayla were excited and overwhelmed with their gifts. They played all day with their new toys. It was such a joy for Karel and I to sit on the couch and admire the family God had blessed us with. I knew we still had a long road to go with Kayla, but I felt that God was watching over her.

The calendar rolled over to 1996 and we were praying for a much quieter year. We spent the first week of the New Year making plans to make Kayla's birthday the following weekend extra special. With her approaching her first birthday, she was finally starting to stand up now on her own. She was still a little wobbly, but after what she had been through, we were just thankful to see her happy and growing.

The year started out with a lot of snow. Throughout the week we received more measurable snowfalls. Although Kayla's birthday is on January 9th, we decided to celebrate it on Sunday the 7th. My parents came over the night before and spent the night, so my mom could help Karel prepare for the party. The next day, Karel's entire family arrived. Even though Kayla did not like the personal size cake that Karel had made just for her, she had a great day with everyone. Given all the snow, Clayton had an extra week off of school, so we went ahead and celebrated again on her actual birthday. Kayla clearly felt very special with all the attention she is receiving.

Later that month, I found that I had an opportunity to transfer my employment closer to where we were originally from, closer to both Karel's and my parents. The job would not be available until May or June. Making the decision to move our family would be bittersweet. It would be hard to move away from all of the relationships we had developed over the past few years. Many of these people had helped us through our struggles after Kayla got sick. But, the opportunity to move closer to family would be the best thing we could hope for. Also, it would be an hour and a half closer to Kayla's doctors in St. Louis. I made notification that I would like to be considered for the position, giving us some time to think and pray about this.

In February, we began to grow concerned that Kayla's left eye was starting to weep more. It happens to be on the same side as her original infection. I found I would be getting the new job effective May 16. We put our house up for sale on March 11. It was such a great feeling, when I came home to find Kayla not only standing up but walking. We know she was behind where she should have been as she was still much smaller than other children her age, but the site of seeing her walk was overwhelming.

We had so many exciting things to tell Dr. Chu when we took her to St. Louis on March 18. They did their examination, started an IV, put in a feeding tube for contrast and took her for a CT. One positive thing about testing in St. Louis was that we always knew the results before we ever left the hospital. Dr. Chu came in and told us that everything looked normal and she was doing well. He told us with childhood cancer, if there is not a reoccurrence within the first year, the likelihood of it reoccurring is rare. He shared our concerns with the weeping and appearance of her left eye, so he immediately scheduled an appointment with Dr. Shields at Anheuser-Busch Eye Institute.

Dr. Shields examined her eye and checked the pressure. After running some additional tests, he broke the news to us that Kayla had Congenial Glaucoma in her left eye. He explained that there are two canals through the eye. If the canals become plugged, it increases pressure inside the eye. We told him about the infection she had when she started this journey over a year ago. He thought that infection was likely the start of it since we did not have any family history of Glaucoma. He said surgery would be necessary to alleviate the pressure.

The surgery was scheduled for April 1. Dr. Chu called and started her on eye drops to keep the pressure down in her eye until surgery. On March 31, we spent the day with my Grandmother to celebrate her 96th birthday. My uncle Eugene mentioned Kayla's surgery on her eye during the table prayer. We spent the night before her surgery at my parents since we had to have her at the hospital at 8:00 am. She went into surgery around 10:30 am and was in recovery until 1:30 pm. When she came out, her eye was covered, and she had an I.V. in her neck. It was like reliving things all over again. She did not do well through the night. Every time she got to sleep, they had to come in and take her vitals.

They took off the patch the following day to reveal that her eye was completely red. They told us the surgery was a success and the redness would take a few days to go away. She soon got the I.V. removed also. Dr. Shield wanted to watch her one more night and she was sent home the following day. We were so excited to have the surgery done and was going to spend Easter with the kids at home. But after being two days home from the hospital, Kayla started vomiting. We took her to the Emergency Room in Vincennes, IN. With her history, they decided to admit her. The doctor in the emergency room also felt that she had an ear infection. Upon checking she also had low blood sugar. We spent Easter in the hospital.

I had to call Dr. Shield's office in St. Louis and cancel her appointment. Kayla ended up staying five days in the hospital this time. On the following Monday, we took her to St. Louis for her post-op exam of her eye. Dr. Shields looked at the eye and said that it looked good. Two days later we headed the other direction for follow-up in Vincennes with her pediatrician from her hospital stay. She was still not feeling well, but not bad enough to be in the hospital. Through all of this we were still trying to keep up our house for showing and looking for new homes closer to my new job. It was all just too much so we decided to get a realtor to list our house. We also managed to find a house that really suited our needs. Kayla also had an appointment with her pediatrician and is doing good again. It seems like everything is starting to do good again.

On May 13th, we headed out to St. Louis for a check-up with Kayla's eye doctor, Dr. Shields. They sedated her, so they could check the pressure in her eyes. They found that her pressures were normal, and that the Glaucoma is gone. He also shared with us her optic nerve had somehow miraculously healed. He said that was not normal as optic nerve damage is permanent. He had no answers how it could have occurred. I know though what healed it, the power of prayer. We had not stopped praying for God to heal her since we first went to the hospital with her well over a year ago.

He told us that he would be fitting her with glasses and recommended patching her good eye to make her bad eye work harder. We picked out some cute little frames. It was amazing how they found the proper prescription for her lenses. The chart had items on it for children to identify that could not read a letter chart. Kayla was only sixteen months old, so it worked well for her. It was the cutest thing when she was able to make out the image of the duck and quacked hysterically to acknowledge what it was she was looking at.

On May 22nd, we made a final offer on the house that we had found pending sale of our house. We then received an offer on our house which we accepted. The pendulum was shifting back up and things were continuing to fall into place. Kayla was doing so well and things were also coming together for our family to relocate to where my new job was. Kayla had scheduled doctor's visits with her pediatrician and they all the blood tests were coming back good. As a family we suffered some setbacks. We had to turn down our house we were buying because the sale of our house fell through. We did not let this get us down. We had been through a lot harder times.

In July, we went back to see Dr. Chu. He did blood tests and x-rays on Kayla. Everything was normal. He scheduled us to come back again in three months for her next check-up. We were so thankful with the care she has been receiving at Cardinal Glennon. Kayla, Karel and I were practically celebrities with the staff in the clinic. They made us feel special. We were on a first name basis with the nurses and even some of the other families and their children. Some of the children were recovering well like Kayla, while others were not doing as good. Over the past year, we spent so many hours in the hospital and overheard several parents receive bad news on their children and watched them break down in tears much as I had done when we handed Kayla over the surgeons and watched them wheel her down the hallway. I prayed that God grant the same healing to them as he granted to us.

In August, things were going so well, we decided to take

a short vacation together as a family. We decided to go to Branson, MO. On the way, we stopped at Bass Pro Shop in Springfield. We went through the Wildlife Museum. It was so cute, Kayla thought everything there was a cow and made mooing sounds. The highlight of the trip was easily when Kayla got to meet Shari Lewis and her famous puppet Lamb Chop. Kayla watches her on TV all the time and got to take pictures with her and get her very owned autographed Lamp Chop.

We finally found another house in Brownstown, Illinois, that a friend of mine had for sale that would be a perfect location for my new job, family and Kayla's doctors. We talked about it and decided to put in an offer. We also had an offer on our house from a family that had been taking their daughter back and forth to St. Jude's in Memphis, Tennessee fighting her own battle with Leukemia. We were able to close on our new house in Brownstown on October 1st. We offered to rent our house to them while they got their financing to help us make payments on the new home. We were having a difficult time finding a suitable offer and given what they were going through with their daughter, it made total sense for us to rent the house and collect enough money for the mortgage on the new home. Their financing ended up falling through. We decided to allow them to rent the house until we could find another buyer.

With the move came yet another new pediatrician for Kayla. Karel took her over for her first check-up and everything went well. On Oct 28th, we made our first trip back to see Dr. Chu after our move. He was delighted to see Kayla's progress and was excited to hear about all the changes we're undertaking as a family. While we were in the elevator taking Kayla to x-ray, there was a team of doctors with us. I recognized one of the doctors. It was Kayla's surgeon, Dr. Silan. I noticed him really staring at Kayla. As we stepped off the elevator, he turned and said, "Kayla Black, left Adrenal Carcinoma Tumor". I was so impressed that he remembered her. He said he continued to follow all of his patients that he performed surgery on. He told us that all the doctors around the hospital knew who Kayla Black was as he had gained notoriety for his successful procedure on her a year and a half earlier. He gave her a hug and even took a few pictures before we departed. All of this seemed so personable.

All the tests came back excellent. Dr. Chu told us that he wanted to write an article for publication in a medical journal on Kayla's progress, with our permission. We consented to it. We were told that she was the longest living patient that Cardinal Glennon Hospital has ever had that survived from an Adrenal Carcinoma Tumor. Usually, the tumor returns in other parts of the body. With Kayla's tumor, it was attached to the adrenal gland and the adrenal vein, which meant there was a high likelihood that the cancer cells were in her blood stream and could easily spread to other parts of her body. The fear was that the cells would stop in her lungs causing lung cancer. This was extremely hard to hear at the time, but, by the grace of God, none of the cells did what was anticipated.

Kayla was a happy, healthy and vibrant little girl. Church, faith and prayers were helping us get through the struggles. Some people have turned away from God during the rough times in their lives. They sometimes want to blame God for their problems. We never blamed God, instead we turned to God asking for his support. I frequently asked him to keep me strong, to give me the strength to handle what we were going through. 1 Chronicles 16:11 says, "Seek the LORD and his strength; seek his presence continually". This is a verse that I have tried to live by, not only for myself, but also for my family.

It was still a struggle owning a house an hour and a half away that we were trying to sell and caring for the house we lived in all while continuing to worry about Kayla's continued improvement and Clayton adjusting to a new school mid-semester. Our contract with the realtor expired and we were contemplating what we should do. The realtor called and said there was an offer on the house. While thinking about the offer, we had a young couple call us wanting to see the house. I made the trip over to show it to them. After months of the house sitting on the market, we had two offers. Since our contract with the realtor had expired, we accepted the private offer. They secured their financing and we finally sold our old house. This was definitely going to ease some of the pressure we had.

Closing became an issue, because the house was rented. The family that was renting had to go to St. Jude's Children hospital as their daughter was struggling with complications from Leukemia. Fortunately, I knew their family from work, so, I contacted them. They were kind enough to decide to move their items out so the closing on the house could move forward the following day. I went over and worked on a few things on the house that need to be repaired before closing. Closing then went as planned and the burden of two houses and two mortgages had been lifted.

It was the spring of 1997 and my grandmother was turning 97 years old. It was always easy to remember how old she was, since she was born in 1900. She was a beautiful lady with the sweetest heart. She impressed upon her family the importance of church and having God in our lives. As the mother of six boys and one girl, her faith carried throughout the family. She had two sons that went on to become Methodist ministers. Her other children held positions in their churches. The time spent with all of them was so enlightening. They said they couldn't believe that she was the same sick little girl they had seen a year ago.

The scheduling in St. Louis always sets up an appointment after my grandmother's birthday. A new doctor had started seeing Kayla. He told us he read her entire chart and was familiar as to who she is and what she had been through. He did his exam and told us she would be having a renal ultrasound due to previous testing showing her left kidney was smaller. We got good news on the kidney. While, the kidney was substantially smaller, it was functioning as it should. Although having a new doctor always made us a bit nervous, the fresh set of eyes often meant a new frame of reference and we would typically hear something new, positive or negative, that we had not heard before.

After we got home we found out that my grandmother, who we just celebrated with, was in the hospital in poor condition. They eased her immediate pain by starting her on medication for congestive heart failure which made her breathing a lot easier. She did not show a lot of improvement though the week and recognizing her age and fragility, we knew that her remaining time on earth was likely limited. Knowing we were about to lose her, we took both kids to see her. She was so excited to see Clayton and Kayla. We visited only for a short time. Both kids hugged her and gave her a kiss before we left. We knew that would be the final time either of them would probably get to see her. I could be at peace knowing that when she passed, she would be reuniting with my grandfather.

The doctors told the family that there was not really anything else they could do for her. They said her 97-year old body and heart were simply wearing out. They worked with the family to get her moved to a nursing facility. The family told her what was going to happen and why. Grandma instead told them that she wanted to go be at home with "dad". The whole family thought she was reliving her youth when in fact she meant she was going home to be with my grandpa. When she referenced home, she was referring to heaven.

I got the phone call from my dad that grandma had

passed away before they could even move her. We got comfort with knowing she passed peacefully. Kayla had become a tremendous part of my Grandmother's life and gave her a reason to hang on. Each time we saw her, she always said how she was still praying for Kayla. We met up with family and went to her visitation. The visitation, while somber, was also a celebration of her life. Everyone that loved her got to say their final farewell to her. I served as a pallbearer. It was one of the greatest honors of my life, getting to take her to her final resting place.

My biggest regret was that Kayla will not remember my grandmother or the Karel's grandmother that she was named after. Although Kayla would not remember them, we took solace in knowing that they had played such a huge role in Karel and I's lives and had helped us grow into the people that we were. They were by our side through the hardest part of our lives from that moment in February 1995 when we got the bad news on Kayla until the moment they left this world. We got comfort in John 14:1-4, "Do not let your hearts be troubled. You believe in God[a]; believe also in me. My Father's house has many rooms; if that were not so, would I have told you that I am going there to prepare a place for you? And if I go and prepare a place for you, I will come back and take you to be with me that you also may be where I am. You know the way to the place where I am going."

In August we took Kayla for two doctor's appointments. We had one scheduled at the Anheuser-Busch Eye Institute and the other at Cardinal Glennon. Dr. Shields told us that her vision was continuing to improve. The only thing that Dr. Chu wanted to do was a chest x-ray. They continued to keep an eye on her lungs since there was a possibility of the cancer returning there. The x-ray was clear. Again, our prayers were being heard and answered.

Dr. Chu told us he was going to reduce her visits from four visits to only twice a year. We were delighted to hear that news. We decided to celebrate by taking both kids to the zoo and Chuck E. Cheese for dinner. The majority of the next several months were life as usual. Kayla again had some recurring episodes of vomiting. We took her to the doctor, but no hospital stay was required because of her age. She would take fluids to keep her hydrated.

We had a teacher coming to the house to do some testing on her. Because of her illness and her glasses, she was being tested for the Kindergarten Readiness Program where we live. Testing revealed she was qualified. She was to start half days. She thought she was a big girl now since she would get to go to school like Clayton.

As the Christmas season started rolling around, Kayla was really getting excited. She couldn't wait to see Santa Claus. She was getting old enough to have a better understanding of the holiday season. She really enjoyed her gifts and seeing everyone. I think everyone enjoyed seeing both kids as well. Kayla had an eye appointment. Her left eye was doing so well that her vision had actually improved in the eye. Because we had been putting a patch over her good right eye, it was helping her left eye develop. The doctor ordered her a new set of frames and lenses. It was incredible how well she had adjusted to wearing them, but between her growing and the wear and tear of a three-year-old with glasses, it was definitely time to replace them. We had also grown up from the animal noises from her initial eye exam to saying what it was she was looking at. Dr. Chu told us that she was doing so well that he would see her again in six months.

The county fair was coming up the first part of July. We decided to let her participate in the Little Miss Pageant. We took her shopping for a little pageant dress. She started going to the practices leaning how to do the walking and the little queen wave. She was so cute practicing for her big night. She learned the dance routine and was practicing a list of potential pop questions. Her big night arrived. She confidently walked across the stage waving to the crowd without an ounce of shyness. For her pop question, they asked her what she wanted to be when she grew up. Kayla's answer was "a Mom". The crowd just loved her, and she ended up winning first runner-up. We were so proud. Tears flowed from our eyes from the joy of seeing her happiness with her little sash and crown. She won several prizes and got to be in numerous parades. She was getting to do the things that other little girls got to do.

Kayla after winning First Runner- up at the
Fayette County Little Miss Pageant.

In August, we had another appointment scheduled at Cardinal Glennon. We had done photographs of her with her dress, sash, crown and trophy she won. We printed one for Dr. Chu to put on his wall. When he saw it, he smiled and gave her a big hug. He did a routine examination of her. He also wanted to do a chest x-ray to check her lungs. It was negative for any issues as it had been for every x-ray before it. He surprised us with the news that he did not need to see her for a year. He told us to call for her next appointment. He told us he still wanted to continue seeing her just to be safe, but did not feel there was any danger of a reassurance of the tumor.

By this point, it had been almost four and a half years since the discovery of her illness and subsequent surgery. Kayla had endured so many setbacks but fought through everything. We can truly understand what God meant in 1 Chronicles 16:34, "Give thanks to the LORD, for he is good; his love endures forever!" When we moved back to Brownstown, we made friends with our new minister. He had a saying, "God is good all the time, All the time God is Good". The following months started to fly by. Time was passing us by faster than we realized.

As the months and years passed, we continued with her yearly check-ups. We asked Dr. Chu how long he wanted to continue seeing her. He told us that the hospital had made a case study on her. He said he would like to see her as long as she was willing. Every time we get the news that everything is good.

One day, Kayla found her scar and started asking about it. Without going into detail, we told her that she had a boo-boo that the doctors took out. We were sure that answer would not be sufficient forever. There would be a time when we would have to dig in and try to explain in greater detail what she had been through. When the time comes, we will dig deep to try to explain it to her. We will make sure that she gets all the answers to her questions. We will tell her, "Jesus laid his hands upon you and made you healthy again". We will share with her that everything is good now, thanks to God.

I will always remember her first day of school. It was a monumental day. She climbed up the steps of the school bus with her brother and off they went to Kindergarten. Her brother Clayton was so protective of her and she looked up to him so much. There were some concerns that she would be behind entering school because of her earlier struggles. Those thoughts were soon put to rest. Kayla began thriving in school, earning exceptional grades from her teachers. In addition to her schoolwork, Kayla's teachers commented positively on her communication skills. She was such a well behaved little girl. To this day, I admit that I never had to scold her for anything because she never did anything wrong. She had her Daddy wrapped around her little finger. All she must do is look at me with those beautiful blue eyes, blonde curls and that sweet smile to get practically anything she wanted.

As her school years progressed, she continued to make the honor roll. Kayla started developing a strong personal relationship with God. She was always excited when the week rolled over to Sunday and we went to Church and Sunday School. She got a copy of a children's bible and started reading it as soon as she was able. She learned to sing Christian songs at an early age. She would always volunteer to sing solos in church.

The first time she really heard the story of her early life was when I read a story I had written about her at the county's annual Relay for Life. I struggled to tell her story, but seeing her standing there served as all the inspiration I needed. I discovered that day, that my little girl was my hero.

When she got into Junior High she asked us about joining a youth music group called "Impact". "Impact" was a music group made up of Jr. High and High School youth in the Methodist Church in Vandalia, Illinois. In the small Methodist church that we were attending at the time, there were not a lot of opportunities for church youth activities, so, we changed churches to make it easier for her to participate.

Through Impact, Kayla went on a couple tours out of state to perform. She went to Atlanta, Georgia, and Branson, Missouri. She performed at juvenile detention facilities, churches, orphanages and several other places. While still in Junior High, she was confirmed and became a member of the church. She continued to prosper in her classes and made high honors with her grades every quarter and received numerous recognitions for being an outstanding student. She participated in cheerleading all through Junior High. We just made a few more visits to Cardinal Glennon Hospital through Junior High. After Junior High she did not want to go over there anymore. We were not going to force her anymore. She was at the age now that she needs to be part of the decision.

Entering high school, it became so apparent that she was truly going to be someone special. She continued with her cheerleading and became her class president. She prospered in all of her academic classes.

Kayla as a Senior in High School

It was not always easy for her, but she put in the extra hard work to achieve the biggest return. She graduated as Valedictorian of her class. She received a full scholarship to attend Lakeland College in Mattoon, IL. When she was younger, she always said she wanted to be a nurse. She ended up having a great love for children and decided instead to go to school for Elementary Education. She received an award for being the top education student at her community college, was president of the education club at the college and graduated with Summa Cum Laude honors.

She decided to continue her education at Greenville College. Greenville College is a Christian College based on Free Methodist principles and was known for being one of the top Education Colleges around. While there, she put in two years of hard work that paid off. Kayla graduated with a Bachelor's Degree in Elementary Education. She even had a teaching job lined up before she graduated. Kayla had been dating her boyfriend Eddie for several years. One night he showed up and asked me for permission to marry my little girl. I agreed to give my blessings. They set a date of June 24th, 2017.

My girl had her work cut out for herself. She had her student teaching to do the semester before the wedding. Kayla also had to complete her Ed. T.P.A., which is the licensing process that the State of Illinois requires to become a teacher. Then there was a wedding to plan. One of the first steps in planning the wedding was of course finding the right dress. She wanted her daddy to be there when she picked it out to give his approval. She tried on several dresses and there was no question when she came out in the right one. She looked so beautiful in it.

When I saw it, it was like time had turned back. I started seeing vivid images of her growing up. I could see her in the hospital bed, fighting for her life. I saw her in our rear-view mirror on one of our countless drives across Illinois to her doctors in Missouri and Indiana. I saw her in that pageant dress and her graduation gowns. And now I realized that my beautiful baby girl had grown into a beautiful young lady. She asked what I thought. I fought back tears and nodded my head. The sales lady asked her if she was saying yes to the dress. She smiled so beautifully and looked me in the eye and said yes and rang the bell.

The coming months were filled with shopping trips for wedding supplies, planning the schedule and booking DJ's, photographers, and venues. Kayla decided to get married in Eddie's small country Christian church. It was going to be a beautiful setting for her beautiful day. We bought all the decorations and found a decorator for the reception. Every time she wanted something, all she would have to do was to look at me and give me "the look". I could not say no to anything. I wanted to do all I could to make the day as perfect for her as the life she helped to give me by being my girl. Everything was planned, and it was all coming together. We went over everything to ensure we had it right. We had the rehearsal planned on the evening before the wedding. I could tell Kayla was going to be a great teacher from the way she had taken charge of her special day, from giving out instructions to her wedding party and ensuring everything and everyone was where they needed to be. She had more control of herself than I did. I was so nervous. This was a time for reflection on everything on my part. I did not know how I could walk her down the aisle and give her away. A friend told me not to make eye contact with anyone. The next morning, Karel left early to go to the church to get hair and make- up done at the church. I spent the morning relaxing, preparing for the big day. While I had some quiet time, I found myself thinking this was the final chapter, my baby was all grown up. She was leaving the nest to start a life of her own.

While I realize the following scripture is known as the wedding verse, it also can also apply to the love we feel for Kayla and the love she felt for us. 1 Corinthians 13:4-8 says, "Love is patient, love is kind. It does not envy, it does not boast, it is not proud. It does not dishonor others, it is not self-seeking, it is not easily angered, it keeps no record of wrongs. [6] Love does not delight in evil but rejoices with the truth. It always protects, always trusts, always hopes, always perseveres. Love never fails. But where there are prophecies, they will cease; where there are tongues, they will be stilled; where there is knowledge, it will pass away."

So, I realized that I was not losing my girl, I was just watching her grow up into a beautiful woman with a full life ahead of her. We headed for the church. When we got there, Kayla was in the church basement getting dressed. She had me sent for when she was dressed. I walked down the steps and turned down the hallway toward her. She had her back turned but was waiting for me. She turned around and smiled. She was absolutely beautiful. Tears came to both of our eyes. I gently hugged her and gave her a light kiss on the cheek. She told me, "I love you Daddy". I will never forget that moment as long as I live. I told her I loved her too. I went upstairs and waited to walk her down the aisle. The wedding was beautiful. Afterwards, everyone headed to the reception. I got to do a father daughter dance with her. My little girl was a married woman.

Kayla and her wonderful husband, Eddie on their wedding day.

In August, she started her teaching job as a first- grade teacher. The kids just love her, and she loves them as well. Her love of God is visible in watching with the ways she lives her life. Since getting married, she attends church regularly and is a member of her church's worship team serving as a song leader. She has the voice of an angel.

It has now been 23 years since that beautiful baby girl was born. We took a journey with her. That ride has been back and forth across the state of Illinois several times. We learned a lot about ourselves along the way.

We found that God was in charge throughout the entire journey. We did and continue to put our confidence and faith in him. God is in control of all things. He guided us to Cardinal Glennon Hospital to seek care for her. It was him that assisted the doctors in finding her problem and providing the proper care. He continued to lead the way in the healing process that enabled us to take her home and care for her. Without God in control, none of this would have been possible.

We try not to, but on occasion we think a lot of what could have been if we had not been persistent about taking her to St. Louis. The thought of what the doctors told us in St. Louis still sticks in our minds. They explained because of her blood pressure, she wouldn't have lived more than two more weeks. She would have very likely suffered a stroke and it would have more than likely been considered a case of Sudden Infant Death Syndrome (SIDS), with them never learning about the tumor on her adrenal gland. We have no idea if the articles or videos that were made about her were ever used to save a life, but that never would have been possible without God's guidance.

We were guided by God to seek help. Psalm 25:4-5 tells us, "Show me your ways, Lord, teach me your paths. Guide me in your truth and teach me, for you are God my Savior, and my hope is in you all day long." The hardest thing we endured was the day we were told, "Your daughter has cancer."

Dr. Chu was right when he said sometimes the unknowns are good and he felt the unknowns were good in Kayla's case. I thank God every day that we got to meet that man and he became Kayla's doctor. I really don't know where we would be today if it were not for him.

Even though, my Uncle Eugene has now passed away, he knew what he was saying on Kayla's surgery day in the Cardinal Glennon waiting room when he told me that God had a special plan for Kayla. Uncle Eugene's words will never leave me.

Kayla's life has been full of good things including the relationships we had with all the hospital and clinic staff. Many of them prayed with us and cried with us. We think about all the friends and family that stood by our side through all the years. We still reflect on the loved ones lost to this terrible disease and we salute those that have fought it to the bitter end. I think about other loved ones that are no longer here that helped make my wife and I become the parents we are today.

We have tried our best to pass these things to Kayla as well. I think about what our son went through for the month Kayla was in the hospital. Clayton was just 6 years old when Kayla became sick. Our home was three hours from the hospital. He stayed so strong because he loved his little sister so much. Their love for each other still shows today.

It was wonderful having my dad able to take vacation time to move into our house to care for Clayton. It enabled him to be able to continue in school and helped him develop a bond with Clayton that they still have today. Would not want to know how we would have handled this time in our lives without the shoulders of our parents to lean and cry on.

There is an old saying that something good can come from anything. There has been a lot of good come from all of this. Primarily, it brought our family closer to God. Kayla's case is being used as a case study that doctors can refer to in caring for other kids with the same disease. It is a hope that more children can live through this disease because Kayla did. It is also my hope that this experience can give both spiritual and emotional support to other parents going through a similar situation. One must put your full confidence in God. Pray for comfort for your child and ask for God to lay his healing hand on them. Ask him for guidance to keep you strong for your child and the rest of the family as well. Remember the other children too. A cancer diagnosis affects the entire family. Stay strong as a family. I thank God every day for the emotional support that he gave me, and most of all, I thank him for giving me my little girl.

About the Author

Michael Black is retired after 29 years from the Illinois Department of Corrections. During his off time, he has worked part-time for ambulance services, served as a volunteer fireman and served as a deputy coroner in the county he currently resides. He volunteered as a 4-H leader, and ran his own photography studio for several years. His proudest moment in life though are the years he has spent as being a father to two wonderful children, Clayton now 28 and Kayla, 23. Having lived the experience in the book with his wife Karel, Mike recently felt a calling to put the journey into this book as a way of giving hope and inspiration to others.

Printed in the United States
By Bookmasters